STRANGER IN TOWN

CITY LIGHTS SPOTLIGHT SERIES NO. 4

CEDAR SIGO

STRANGER

IN

TOWN

CITY LIGHTS

SAN FRANCISCO

CITY LIGHTS SPOTLIGHT
The City Lights Spotlight Series was founded in 2009, and is
edited by Garrett Caples, with the assistance of Maia Ipp.

Library of Congress Cataloging-in-Publication Data
Sigo, Cedar.
Stranger in town / Cedar Sigo.
p. cm. — (City Lights spotlight series ; no. 4)
ISBN 978-0-87286-536-5
I. Title. II. Series.
PS3619.I473S77 2010
811'.6—dc22
2010018534

Cover Image: Will Yackulic, *Foil Plotting New Illusion* (detail)
Cover image copyright © 2010 by Will Yackulic

All City Lights Books are distributed to the trade by
Consortium Book Sales and Distribution: www.cbsd.com

For small press poetry titles by this author and others,
visit Small Press Distribution: www.spdbooks.com

City Lights Books are published at the City Lights Bookstore,
261 Columbus Avenue, San Francisco, CA 94133
www.citylights.com

This book is for my family

Acknowledgments

Special thanks to: Johnny Huston, Garrett Caples, Will Yackulic, Micah Ballard, Sara Bilandzija, Corina Bilandzija, Frank Haines, Nathan Berlinguette, Colter Jacobsen, Julien Poirier, Seth Bogart, Joanne Kyger, Donald Guravich, Michael Slosek, Noel Black, Kevin Opstedal, Josefa Perez, Duncan McNaughton, Bill Berkson, Kevin Killian, Tomo Yasuda, David Enos, Margaret Tedesco, Darin Klein, and Jonathan Brun.

Some of these poems appeared in the following publications: *String of Small Machines*, *The Can*, *Morning Train*, *Blue Book*, *Greetings*, *Viz*, *Canteen*, *Capilino Review*, *Night Palace*, *Try*, *Pressed Wafer*, *Bolinas Hearsay News*, *Big Bell*, *Currency*, *Cannibal*, *21st Century Queer Artists Identify Themselves*, and *Pax Americana*; in the following chapbooks: *Plywood Press Primer* (2001), *Goodnight Nurse* (Angry Dog, 2001), *Stranger in Town* (Auguste Press, 2007), *Expensive Magic* (House Press, 2008), *Portraits* (Box of Books, 2009), and *Music for Torching* (Lew Gallery, 2010); on the broadside *Zen with a Lisp* (2nd Fl. Projects, 2008); and in the books: *The Blind See Only This World: Poems for John Wieners* (Granary Books / Pressed Wafer, 2000) and Oscar Tuazon, *I Can't See* (Paraguay Press / Do.pe., 2010).

CONTENTS

STRANGER IN TOWN

PRINCE VALIANT

Your first presence
is that of a con man
down on his luck.
You cross on the ferry
and return
as it gets dark.
Heating a pair
of candlesticks
to warm the studio
I was to live
quite comfortably
at the end
of each needle
to receive my ghost
I took out
a writing room also
among derelicts
who would pay
unwittingly
the highest prices

besides the apartments
for their dry cleaning
and drinks,
TOP OF THE MARK
soiled by each groom
till I reach the morgue,
One we can lean on
in our ascension
to heaven
to CHINA FIELDS
and the cufflinks
You had better
recognize
It was more
of an open invitation
and should
he care to appear,
good thing it was recorded.
His walking seaside,
His being punished
for talking Indian.
A bronze bust
soon to be unveiled

in PIONEER SQUARE
The greatest
of all features
in its design . . . Mercy
the brass ring
and clear purple tomb
in a door knob.

LISBON

I get so
tired at times
and thank

all of
the pills
for being

themselves
and the men
I thank as many

as I bring
to mind again
Fine lines

wander the top
of the stairwell
also in my place

A gaslight
desk set
stagecoach

Blueprints
for imperial
washrooms

Arrows longing
for the
other bank

DAYBREAK STAR

Twice wrongly accused
I had wandered into the booth
to be alone,
Every morning
the black sunrise,
gay shame awards,
I write more letters
suspicion is heightened
by the wording
& my ability to relax.
I shall be made
thy music
since I shut the doors
on this
holy room,
just got a big fine
leather chair
& copy of FORTUNE
(I've worked all my life.)
had stumbled off

from the lighthouse
       & had my choice
more rooms
than I had time,
    It was one of my best comes
Identical
      To such new luxury
the marsh banks
keep it small, I appreciate
its stable & its manor
its drowned exile, flight
to what restless longing
     The films and tapes
& cinemascopes
I screened all together
  & typed out a list
THINGS I FIND EXTINCT
The audience, my own
a higher order
     with whom
I would consent to learn
read, converse, never this building
a replica world.

This is my test
of the ink, the privacy
in composition prized.

SPEEDWAY

FOR JOHN WIENERS

I cut out the "Heart with Snowflake"
Myself but it is not mine, Forget
This bloody coat bloody shirt, I
Think it is the writing that makes
Me sick, The scores and scores of
Incidental music, this nosebleed all
Spring all wet, I'm positively angry
with the Impertinence of it! I'm
Sewing up the kinks in this film, I'm
Trying to! I'm trying to burn a light
Between, There's a light and I cable
my voice on it but it rips when I trace
Anything! WORKS ON PAPER, THE SHIP
OF DEATH "Oh build it!" Sings the
Heart, "My coat would be so bloodied
I could wiggle out of my coat!"

SERIOUSLY UNDERDRESSED

Acid washed

Jeans, bitten down

Fingernails, I've been

Uptight all

This week wishing

Invisibility,

Scented tissue

I can tease

Into flowers, same

As ever My heart-shaped collapsible

Locket is still

Missing & I miss

Wearing it open,

I remember a black

Fog inside so

Combed through, trapped

And willingly

Shining me on

PORT ORCHARD

When the song birds arrive

liquormen of the world
     will squirm
      & snarl
      & scheme
It is more about
    what the ROOM wants

I wish she were Duke Wayne

But with face and figure

    willingness to come apart
   smoke up
       &
         drink down
  To be a con man
is   gathering dust

drifting in &
changing then
the walk of
the little town

us purple hearts just care for
that passing life (Lives)
I am growing to love the wait

"fancy" a toss. What is the
cost   to drink in
the other room?

A first born son, one silver
Piece,
A wedding
under chandelier
in DARK COMMAND.

LIVE AT THE EAST

These tears
      bury
They have been
    left out
in Hades' sun

    Patterns in
music I once
      found difficult
    to distinguish

Now repeat
      themselves
in fire and
   kiss the ring

    connecting
    passages
to the black
   vaults

and crowned heads
of the
coral seas, the edges
of their
collars

had onyx scaled
to amber
The dust
that we wish
to gather against.
That would flash
on me still

The writing's
already
a tape already
revolving

with jewelry
cleaners
concentrate
Make light so

          pained
No smoke
          in the
          lungs.

JOHN ALTOON

The neck
of the flask
pitch black-getting bored
jacked
also madness, insidious
intended ghost
(days late)
I cross green & white flowered seas
Valentines, May Day
conferring with henchmen
one must keep holy
the edges of fragments
slots used
clothes loose
dried bloodspots
bolster elegance
Found a goldmine
outside a mansion
a prolongation
of the art

of very rich hours

oil in

childe ballads

sung, unsung against I should say

"over" though,

The Cosmos

slows it for us

The heretofore unmentioned

26th Series

(he gets the girl)

sparks fall   call me

if you do die

STRANGER IN TOWN

Life in
    unbridled

      collapse, Let tuneful praise ascend

          Not a single line

        out of step with my band, aboard

       the riverboat
    when the sun
        shown red

and especially dark upon my room

            I was shown

              to 3464

             once Jack Lon
              dons

I was told.

The black forest alcohols

filled my mind, my one & only skull

with rock crystal
(The Butchers Field)

Its grass &

the stream

cut my rooms in 3. I write & I laugh

to think again upon the stream,

its demon
black mask

lights under-
neath

My servants stay fine
&
lower their eyes
I proclaim the empire, my coat of arms

& cigarettes

to be held across

façades of cathedrals, crimson the flight.

More than one death

from a square

bottled ink

The MARVEL brand

I enjoy reading signs

through the fog——

—HOTEL HUNTINGTON—

Then that evening

and all of

Fox Plaza   was the same white

A permanent

                    stripe
            on my blue bike

          I raise my hood

      I think there are other lost men

in surrounding blocks

                  alike in their thinking

        "There is
               no other man
to enjoy
      such fog
besides me."   to wander tracks

            in clear

          star cut
            ground

I am sorry I said
he was
already high

We got so high together

and I forgot to say

I had invested a lot
in my first
walkthrough

the greatest

Marco
Polo
single file
best roulette
There's a bad moon

on the rise and I've got
quite a stash

rubbings from the calligram

graves,

I have explained their
hollows and brick

a cross where it is written in
script

YOUNG BLOOD STRAIGHT EDGE

Impossibly accurate   the fifth wristwatch

diamond
on the 12

I have reached the cave   it has been
shot up.

& I am punished to this day

ruby under

black

letterpress

My name goes first.

SHOWBOAT

FOR PATRICK DUNAGAN

I thought you were coming toward me

a few blocks earlier

down Hyde St. It was a man weak

and crushed beneath this gray wig

for women. I can't believe that

it's really you. Who would ever

remove both shoes in the Tenderloin?

Waiting outside of LIFETIME BOOKS

I rejected your invitation to the Jack Hirschman

reading, as he was not represented by

top agencies, he had given a reading

at the police station. None of this

concerns the poem as pure entrance,

what I have allowed & what I might do . . .

Fix myself against a long drink, write

out any trace of formal training in praise

of Jack. Go back and visit rulers of the interior.

Let loose our new books and prints

NOTES ON JOAN CRAWFORD

Metro used her real life exposure
to the lower classes

 Her mother was a laundry woman.
It is said that Joan would hand her clothes

from off the line. She fled Texas

   & found immediate
success upon the casting couch. Then
  having landed a spot in a chorus line
    of New York
she was asked to "entertain" executives
    out from Hollywood
  This seemed to open doors & she was
     soon moved to Brentwood
A majority of early vehicles cast her as a little
shop girl—THE WOMEN. She had a string of hits
into the forties, but was suddenly labeled box
office poison & asked to leave Metro.

She would gain her revenge signing with Warners
winning her first & only Best Actress Oscar for MILDRED
PIERCE. She is increasingly showing her age. She once accepted
an Oscar on another woman's behalf & for spite, reportedly beat
the fuck out of two adopted children, owned her own ill-fated
   casino, Vienna's, in JOHNNY GUITAR. She married Albert Steele,
   the magnate
              behind Pepsi-Cola
                      & did remain on its board of directors

after his sudden death.

She ended in B horror. BABY JANE, BERSERK
                 & her last feature TROG (1970?)
She took whatever crumbs were offered on television   one foot
      in the grave. Her last was an episode of NIGHT GALLERY

      She plays blind
      It was Spielberg's first professional job. He has recalled
there being a lot of cue cards used   large type editions

SONG

We had sailors all over town
Living hand over fist upon their royalties.
I would eventually break their key,
Accidentally & by my own foot
There was one beauty there to sing
& another to divorce me,
Tell me I needn't fear, be kind.
He still taps one foot across the Nile
To much acclaim in my own mind
Had the nerve to lay a matchbox
On my clothes, on my sink in my bedroom,
My good life & hard times.

GREENSLEEVES

The confines
of this book
(Vieux Carre)
identical to those
of Napoleon House
wherein it was written
with enough
rooms
dread, falls
vaults
& blades
awesome in
any evening
It is all worth
what is written
now
The House on Straw Hill
I purchased
just to hold
a secret

book safe
So our illustrations
from Old Gold
stay still, dry
& the dream
poem
of Joanne & I
out shopping
Salvation Army
glowing with the rush
of blood, she rose
she had an air
NOTES FROM BIG SUR
& FOREST FLOWER
by Charles Lloyd
Quartet,
A book on
Treblinka
& its uprising
& another called
WORKS IN PROGRESS
A list of straight
nobody except

Chester Himes'
autobiography THE QUALITY
OF HURT
& after we felt
ten stories longer
& saw we were luckier,
both records
both books

MY DRAWINGS

They were usually a series in ordinary blue & black ballpoint pen. The pages of the tablets were slender and tiny. Genies were my first obsessive series. There was never a man or a woman holding the lamp. It was more being able to get the smoke turning into the genie. They were broad-shouldered with golden rings around the bicep and cat's eye mascara. The hair was pulled up into a fountain-head. If I just felt like drawing a beautiful sideways woman & was especially interested in her dress I would just give her two single lines for legs with perfect circles at the ends colored in. I worked on filler paper for my next series, GREEK GODDESSES—I drew only the occasional god. I did all of these in one notebook. JUNO, APHRODITE and my Helen were the most attractive. The noses were all in profile and ran downward. They were one line with a broken corner. I told my mother I believed in all of these goddesses alongside the god I learned at church & she was pissed. I stopped drawing until just recently. I have tried to copy the author portraits in the front pages of classic paperbacks. My Stendhal came out okay & Huysmans & my Francoise Sagan.

PORTRAIT OF SARA BILANDZIJA

Not an utter stillness but one with a sometimes buried sometimes flickering spark. It was only to be uncovered via talk and subsequent closeness. Preparing tea without a tray. The parts one had always wanted a listener for. The words on writing that have been collected by being alone in the middle of its ocean. "When you write a thing it is perfectly clear and then you begin to be doubtful about it, but then you read it again and you lose yourself in it again as when you wrote it." To imagine one's travels someone else's, is the perfect drift for writing. To attempt to remember one's own travels is more likely erasing parts of a favorite picture. If you try and remember the goings on from the moment of landing or docking, a train slowing down and well-wishers gather close to a door still closed. Evenings. There seemed to be new lovers at the end of every get together, mostly arranged through others (involved). They were so often clean and well off demons and enjoyed meeting one another by chance. Their shaking hands and not speaking but smiling devils in the flesh. I felt thin as a rail at that party and that when anyone saw me from the side that my face was in fact flat. My shoulders were tight and my head stuck out brightly from this tightness, attractive—fixing a crooked mirror, crossing the floor, lifting the needle, setting it down, taking a sip, making remarks from another room.

POEM

FOR RYAN KAHL

"Estate with gems"
introduced
as separate pieces
Refinement
I forget the name of his hotel,
AMBASSADOR.
You are asked
To kindly leave
ID with the front desk.
I forgot to take the pill
He promised
I wish I could
Have it with me now
Once inside
We climbed the staircase
And he played the latest
Of his recordings,

"Do not shut your sharp teeth on my pen."

"Do not drink the last of mine."

A GALLOWS GARDEN

The tree has grown
between

the window &
its bars

SAD SERVANT

OF THE INLAND SIDE

gold leaf

bound in vellum

Desiree Justina Fields

You taught me
        the lower case

"l"

        serves for the

        number one

    if it seems

missing again

        (COPY MACHINE)

Alluvial Plains
        Here in this hotel

upon which I typed
earlier drafts from DEATHRACE

Asealingold

I have yet to see.

THE SECRET CEREMONY

"The sources of great events are like those of rivers, in vain do we explore the earth's surface, we can never find them. I cannot say there was any concrete proof of conspiracy with the outer world."

It was a pause in a psychopathic mind I had printed, costly, dismissed as ephemera, "O blessed plain, O pointed chasm," sexy decoy—standard randoms.

It is always an attempt at traction. It is not an open channel. I do not have the choice to wake up & dress & wander beside it by morning.

If ever I do find myself sort of free to wander the grounds, the pain then becomes knowing in due time I'll be escorted out.

Only a reading or dream bears the slightest resemblance. The best trap door & vortex, a relief when I find myself broke & run out of town.

I am beginning to miss all the sad young men choking on their youth.

There are any number of competent singers among poets; too few know to write the arrangements.

I want to bend this note and bend that note, write this way, sing that & get all the feeling, eat all the good foods & sail all around the world in one day.

Of course this tires, too. One must keep holy the edges of fragments, checked in one line checked out the next. A hardened form of the mind turned fluid.

Trimmings. I have a stronger hand after they are charged & coming up for air. I have always enjoyed imposing the order then showing through, thinning the edges.

It can be a sleight of hand or backward sweeps across a phony ballroom. Darktown strutters ball.

The mind has its lines set first thing upstate.

I seem to have escaped the pitfalls of appliqué, chains with anvils, home recordings, blood in blood out, clean-shaven, balanced & steamboat rocks, garden of the gods.

They used to keep a huge ranch out in valley center we used to get wasted on. It defines perfection & is also very limiting.

COLISEUM

You would meet someplace
in private.
There was a format,
and contract
you would almost begin
to write the book together. "Well,
I do need the money."
I've been typing on the other sides
of final
drafts, selling off the atelier
even the herbarium, charms at the end of a
chain, thankfully stamped
such and such
a vintage, priceless crossing
of canals
coats checked
the lamps lowered are lit
and rise again. It helps to settle
into truly eternal
topical matters-technique.

"get out of your own way,
never barricade
the corners" or the
present possibility
of danger, that insistence.
We are starting down
upon the same knife point.
I never think of
catching up to begin with...
triggers on words,
underworld eyes
quiver in tears
Tolstoy/Samurai
delicate planks
that move the characters
literally forward
There is far too much energy
spent elsewhere—
I have to stay interested besides
no dead ends in atmospheric words,
tooth rotten endings.

VILLON

In Paris
        on the hill
where fools are hanged
              & blackened in the wind
        where police (the best pimps)
string up five & six at once
            the greatest cons
are stuck on top
            & feel the nice breeze
       Steer clear of padded cells
a cut purse jerk
with hacked off
          bloody ears is
good as dead
            Watch out for guys like the hangmen

Rush the suits passing by
         count out the cash they've got
               find the open road

and fast
   so they won't stick you
   on that scaffold
      whiter than plaster of Paris
If the cops should catch a glimpse
    keep your wits
    stay calm
just let them have your ass
     & they won't clap you into the irons
Look out for these guys the hangmen

Escape that hook
   they hang the noose from
     or else you'll feel
that loose north wind
     or pass out on haystacks
     in a filthy cell, 4 thick walls
   leave town
   don't act stupid
& their attendants won't have you laid out
drying in the breeze
    Have the guts to cheat
   fill the ears of idiots

                          with perfect lies
              You can fleece them good
              Watch out for guys like hangmen

When you're cracking the safes
     one snitch may not be sleeping
Make sure they don't get wise
     rat you out & change your life
Look out for all the hangmen

$$$EXPENSIVE MAGIC$$$

I stumble down   around torn peaks

"Fit the right suit

to trick them all."

the questions fall

around allure. Poems floated

from the hearth

sparks

out the mouth. I am wound up, bored

we are only strangers on our way

the hotel   turned slender to mind

now written out (sloppy)

to music

dark brown wood

gold mirrors

(tight)

The drinking songs from upper stories

drag us to sleep   a bend in the basement wall

unexplained

scorched, pulling on clean clothes

I let myself out

walk up

underground

to a far off hill

         smoke on top

"The orchestra of the

     immense magnified

inner life

    is now prodigious."

the strings sound down

   Make the surface of a mirror

       & hang the head

  my forbidden past

Rose & Silk

the wine is young

      The brooks still hum

            with melted snow

LONDON, LONDON

Light turned up on the green wall, I was

careful when shaving letting the hairs grow out

till late afternoon. I have done some drinking for sport

nothing that's crippling. Off nights I enjoy a light

solution cognac before bed. The balance of pressure

must be taken up by the skull, every seat filled

in my (too small) theater. Cloth chosen & hung on nails.

Carriage Entrance. The diamonds as I drew them had great

cross-hatching lines both front & back of the range.

I saw a lone flower & wanted the same stray & bloody stripe

mass produced, per request. A simple cut back garden,

split a pot of tea & further my fortune. I could just not

give up all the inanimate, innumerable obsessions. Nor keep on

with the same sorts of poems. Get me my radio

I want to listen to some professional music.

MORNING TRAIN

FOR MICAH BALLARD

I have a room for three nights

It pays me no mind

My lines are columns pulled up

and straight sinking

I begin to see burned in every verse

an alcove, a rest, a bloody lumbering foot

I have cracked the words filled in wine

The song that skirts the ones rehearsing

"part of the old divine threat" exquisite

trailing stains

John has turned on THE BODY SNATCHER by Robert Wise (1945). One man leans over another strangling on his knees, his vest getting tighter toward death, sleeves creeping up. A door closes over black ink, figures stricken with grief, this poor unfortunate mind. A gentleman of consequence who couldn't swallow the shame.

I flip back

      through LOST ILLUSIONS

           Your copy

  skipping of course

his sojourn in the green woods

        & turning straight to SF——

& passing through Mexico

         Tangiers, France & London

    rewritten

His voice is like an ex-husband

        knocking at the door

                  & worth my time again

       Last night trying to put the songs down

                              right ways first

           lost track—just odds & ends to clean up now

      I am strongest

             before the world wakes.

THE EMERALD TABLET

FOR OSCAR TUAZON

6   The Father of all perfection in the whole world is here
7   Its force or power is entire if it be converted into earth

One of my primary concerns in poetry has become the courtship, recognition, and handling of physical tension. Does it die down along the furnished room or become changed by it? (I think of THE LORDLY AND ISOLATE SATYRS, the grip in Charles Olson's line, "only the vault of their being taking rest.") People know you do something, but poetry is often a last guess as to anyone's chosen field. I'm still quite impressed by its plaintive skin and boiling insides, its suited discretion. It is much like whistling down around the catacombs, or worse, tapping one's foot, waiting for remains to surface.

■

Captivity, Constancy, Bright Prospects, Defiance, Wisdom, Lightning Snake, Carefree, Lighthearted, Journey, Courtship, Infancy, Youth, Middle & Old Age, Alertness, Protection, Friendship,

Thunderbird, Sacred Bearer of Happiness Unlimited, Human Life, Peace, Paths Crossing, Warding Off, Feathers, Enclosure, Guarding Good Luck, Watchful, Wise, Sky, Horse, Plentiful Crops, Constant Life, Happiness, Guidance, Morning Stars, Days & Nights, Swiftness, Time, Good Omen, Plenty Game

■

What I was seeing was half a hotel
so I wrote that down to see the picture better

■

After first thinking I would write on resistance, its opposite, compliance, kept pointing out at inopportune angles and moving instantly to work. Is it just a hair that separates disfigured language (in which the words turn away, icing each other out) versus expansive (marrying the world in warm flowing tones of voice)? Each poem was once a separate jewel—they have since been washed into very broad fabric. I have let it roll out and paid the highest price for what many assume to be found pieces. It doesn't feel as if anyone is working over anything to get a desired effect. They were already always doing it. Distinction is the medium, never something sought after. I trace my surface.

■

The section after the quote needs quickening. So much as I also loved the carriage entrance where it was, it turned the section too opaque. The switch from the last line to the first matches the figure moving through the landscape, it gets him going. It is too grand as an ending, but draws the reader into the movement I intend immediately. I like the ending to hinge upon the pairing of "young" and "hum" aloud. When the snow melts it makes a sound. I sacrifice beautiful and resplendent lines in service of the skeleton, i.e. the hand-sanded lens.

SIMPLE GIFT

ON A PAINTING BY BOB THOMPSON

The mouth of the cavern
Is cut along the top like snowy peaks
In cartoons—it zigzags. I sweat onto
My violet shirt in the shape
Of a heart, lock that away
Behind varnish, a hidden floor
Between stalactites
      (long trick knives)
        A lady of Falconbridge & lady
Of Dorset
    Torn back
Through the center & made quiet
A paper cut black branch set
On a red field. A horse
Draws the carriage past a lake
Of blue & all the kinds
    Are laid down

In the forest to live
Tilt their heads back
Don't think of stopping
Your shooting, more drinking!
These are to be
Among the permanent
(wrong) colors
Ice rats in stairwells, above us
Centaurs (twins) smack their heads
Into light bulbs. They get excited
Over massacre
Who were once
The innocents who never hoped
To live out unspoken prayer. A country
That laid dark so long
Pyramids send word
To the painted mountains
Don't try and lie down
As it gets late. Stay on guard
Study your drums & then tighten, pound back
A few shots more
Ash on the sea floors

Don't you scrape away too many organs
Or paint over.

Do not temper the spirit.

THE SUN

Poetry can be a difficult field to enter into, as I find people sometimes think of it as old fashioned. It is this assumption that drives me to try & keep current. I do not just want to interest academics. Skaters are more dear to my heart. Boredom is the cardinal sin. Collaboration can be a terrific introduction to poetry. Things tend to happen a lot faster than they might with a single author. Sometimes I will just be talking my head off while someone else has the typewriter & bits of our conversation will find their way in. It is one of the poet's great fantasies come to life, having a secretary recording over your shoulder & making the words fit rhythmically, too. Often it is the second draft of the poem I look forward to typing (in collaborations & just my own poems). The first draft is a catalogue of content, a list of everything available. The second is more a test of skill & the sounds you wish to make. You may have to sacrifice beautiful & resplendent lines in service of the skeleton. This is not to say there might not be a third possible draft, though for me that could be written out a month later or when I'm asked to contribute to a magazine. It is not always that lines must be removed. It may be that the poem needs one or two added. A lot of my practice is listening. I try & respect that I am making demands on an outside force I do not entirely control. It is more about what the rooms want...or John Wieners once wrote, "and now the season of the furnished room." I wouldn't still be writing if was not more fun than almost anything else & if I wasn't writing poems that I wished to enter over & over again. I do not dwell on my books. They feel like interruptions almost. They are in pursuit of my present obsessions. That is why I demand so much of their physical appearance, so they might stand a chance against the unfinished work in my desk drawer. I feel like all of this reads like conspiracy theory. I can only speak from what I have found, from the poems that I have written so far.

I have tried above all to bring an allure to poetry. Where I would once read other poems to begin my own, now it's more common that I write in response to hearing live music, attending an art exhibit, films, or just going out. When I call to mind all the artists I have met & held dear over the years the lines that divide our fields begin to blur. This seems to me a result of both real dedication & capability. We feel like a band of mystics along the right tracks. Some will be beside you for just a stretch (before they move to Brooklyn). How does one go about distinguishing who is part of this family? I have always returned to the ones that were willing to share their obsessions immediately. Of course there is much discipline involved within the practice of writing, it's not just painting the town red every chance you get. That element is held in check by my voracious reading habit. Are you willing to search for long out of print authors & editions? If you are obsessed with the particulars of a certain author's life or with the deep gossip behind how certain books got printed, this is a good sign that writing is not just an exercise to you, that you've "got it bad." When I first moved to the Mission & established a household (2000), I found it difficult to continue to write my poetry. I was suddenly more calm & contented. I had been leaning on this hysterical tone of voice as if things had to be dark & dissatisfied to be worthy. Someone described my more recent work as pertaining to an urban mysticism. In the best of these poems all surrounding lines slide out at the last possible second. The lines that remain are then shocked into levitation. "Threads of gold fall closely together / Coming to break us off." When I allow a narrative to develop between lines it feels as if I've left open a door to my room, flooding it with outside light. Whenever I slam that door shut (or create a wind to shut it), words turn opaque, more dependent on sound & chance. I wish to hold the listener on a purely subliminal level (never cloying). I am in pursuit of absolute fluency in poetry. I still tend to think of its line as being engraved. The torn strings of words get hanged together & are contingent upon one another. The voice has fit to a measure that begins at the poem's first letter & maybe runs through the rest of your life's work. Ten years in the fully furnished trenches of poetry have given me the confidence to leave a particular word in its place. I seem to know how to climb into a bath & after several days (weeks) climb back out. Jack Spicer speaks well of this total immersion in his "Vancouver Lecture #1"—"If there's no resistance, if the thing saying the thing is exactly what the host wants to say, the host just doesn't have any feeling that he's said anything—it just goes through like a dose of salts." It sometimes takes so long I do admit I am by definition "lording over" the poems, but it feels unconscious. Even if a poem may appear in its first reading to be just odds & ends, it's what the voice has come to. Now it seems that if you don't leave in all of the sleepwalking & nosedives between lines you should just not bother. The nosedives are what interest me most, the uncanny. Someone has been bringing a brand new cut to this line. It already feels so flattering. I won't fit in too much with my former self in writing. I will simply write of the rewards gained by a life in the arts, problem solving declarative sentences.

MUSIC FOR TORCHING

All I see

    in the mirror every morning

        is a face that needs washing

     I've been abroad all my life

     like fantasy land come true

          I have ruled the world

cooling in a bucket beside the bed

       for men only

       don't tell me, tell her

        I can't stand myself (when you touch me)

            loving is really my game

    I didn't know what time it was

        Eden was just like this

The wind is like a movie

     mysterious & drawn out

     It puts me to sleep

     a thousand miles from home

        and I never harmed no one

I was checked in one line
　　　　checked out the next
　　　　　　　pitching the right keys
　　　　　my sensitivity creates technique

　　　　　　　You might not want to speak
　　　　　　　as if you hung the moon

It's high time we sort the killers out
　　　　　from dedicated followers of fashion
　　　　　　　Turning over a new leaf
　　　　　　　giving myself the lion's share
　　　　　　　　　tomorrow is another day
　　　　　　　flying off handle
　　　　Strike me, be cross, but don't hate me!

Hesiod slept under a tree, woke up
　　　　　　　two small waves to drown him deep
　　　　does that seem to hang together?
　　　　The first matter
　　　　　　of the spiritual work

is always within us

A thousand miles from home

I was crushed out

up & down the coast

always out of my Chinese skull

■   ■   ■

Moonlight through quizzing glass

Joe Meek

dance in slush

reduce the uncertainty the people confront

that label comes from outside

I write what is interesting for me to read

Anselm Hollo

Ed Dorn

interesting or not

Mrs. Elaine Feinstein

it really is happenstance in my life

absolute hedonist

read the word
read the next word
I was fortunate in friends
I'll get you a reading
1975-77 San Francisco
Michael Myers
Rolling Stock

The house is still there

I left the Polaroid on my bookshelf in the sun and it was twice
as bright after. It was several years old and I thought the light
had uncovered everything. There was a little paperback book
devoted to Vincent Price's drawing collection, nice reproductions.
I remember one Picasso. I don't know why I didn't pick it up.
It was two dollars at the public library book sale.

I am a dealer of all sorts
anyone's friend's coke is good

flashing   flashing   lights   lights

I messed up this exquisite corpse
      brushing under its nails
      dusting off old tricks
           for the late late show,
           Swindlers in Séance
           Man in a Bottle
  the blackbirds rest
             in a net kept folded
      lying in the dark
        a fleeting single volume
   squared at attention.

   When I speaks
        I speak queens English
          mostly in service of having a drink
        taking a drag
            untaxed accents
            London thugs
    falling down

I am a card,
    a gay blade around women
        treat my ills in other realms
        Transylvania,
          my heart won't erase
  even to an off-tone chamber music
          hath wrath men again
      blowing noon you soon
          hell bent building bid good morning
  Canoe Cologne,
     Alice Coltrane ring tones
         working a white Ike Turner
         male Amelia Earhart

        expected in the lobby
          massive silence
        it turned my one shot into four
           ransacking the rooms,
          transparent prism
  an outline of swamps,

nonchalance
a room abandoned, room in check

My orange on the table
on the rug your clothes
Your breathing in my bed
is sweet and presently a gift
The dark is a cool stone
spark in life

Flash
Fake
Manor
Mist
Surging
Shut
Sun
Small
Shadows
Planks
Entwined

                                Thrown
                                    Atoning
                                        Flows

            One half
            One Page
            Two Poems

            Smoking room, scribbled,

                                    closed.

                        ▪   ▪   ▪

The Modern House of Holland
Tea with whiskey
cheap coffee
A cloud of rain that breaks above Andromeda's suffering
in a long and elegant mystery
a lonely widow takes in a gambler
delicately carved and polished

A kind of book that has been held captive in design
The first of its kind, relaxed and varnished various ways
fold it closed. The actual words dealt in betrayal
being left crying at the vanity combing one's hair night upon night

She despises teenagers and weddings

honeymooners, runaways, vipers, chasing after those in dreams
sure the papers are in order, you are groomed articulate
a catch-not gentleman

The drop has traveled, it's finally reached my eye.

> Plain lead pencil to connect stars
> a sketch is now the highest form
> bearings inexactly set
> registry effectively impossible
> they never gain footing in a style first
> just a show-off trick but it's so slow
> Addict, Thief, Pimp, Pusher, Player, Writer
> accidentally too enamored
> I guess we're making up or

the only way out
is through unnaturally interrupted Hippocrates
when two vectors meet
a third direction forms a track
there's nothing much to be gained
by putting fashion on the dock
it is made and unmade
I rot where you will rot yourselves
red glare of old blood pumping
at first it's charming
It's Mamie Van Doren like, Erica Gavin
high and faint across the canyon
a painful case and grace complete, the dead incomplete

This poem includes contributions from
NATHAN BERLINGUETTE *and* WILL YACKULIC

UNTITLED (NIJINSKY)

Lots to confess, your best interests,
if you are so inclined to backroom
show business memoir, WALKING THROUGH CLEAR WATER
IN A POOL PAINTED BLACK——"I just slip in and out" and
seem to be drawn to a place by folks who don't
know where they want me but I do in fact appear. Then
held over several weeks (backroom)(bloodsucking)(donkey $how)
I once saw a picture of John Wieners arriving to an opening of John
Chamberlain's (twisted) with a not quite long enough ponytail
greased. He appeared to be sleepwalking. I think it was mid-sixties. I
am wearing a more Genet-style sailor's top now, about to run down
to the dock. The fleets come in. I could have had them all along. Ten
years. I've loved you once too hard and twice too soft now. Three
times a lady.

ABOUT THE AUTHOR

Born in 1978 on the Suquamish Indian Reservation in Washington
State, Cedar Sigo studied at Naropa under Anne Waldman, Lisa
Jarnot, and Anselm Hollo. His first book, *Selected Writings* (2003),
was reprinted in a revised edition in 2005. His work also appears in
the books *The Blind See Only This World: Poems for John Wieners*
(2000) and Oscar Tuazon, *I Can't See* (2010). He has collaborated
with many visual artists, including Cecilia Dougherty, Frank
Haines, Will Yackulic, and Colter Jacobsen. A writer on art, litera-
ture, and film, Sigo recently blogged for SFMOMA's Open Space.
Currently, he is guest editing the second issue of *The Can*, a journal
devoted to writing on poetics. He lives in San Francisco.

The state of the world calls out for poetry
to save it. LAWRENCE FERLINGHETTI

CITY LIGHTS SPOTLIGHT SHINES A LIGHT ON THE WEALTH
OF INNOVATIVE AMERICAN POETRY BEING WRITTEN TODAY.
WE PUBLISH ACCOMPLISHED FIGURES KNOWN IN THE
POETRY COMMUNITY AS WELL AS YOUNG EMERGING POETS,
USING THE CULTURAL VISIBILITY OF CITY LIGHTS TO BRING
THEIR WORK TO A WIDER AUDIENCE. IN DOING SO, WE ALSO
HOPE TO DRAW ATTENTION TO THOSE SMALL PRESSES
PUBLISHING SUCH AUTHORS. WITH CITY LIGHTS SPOTLIGHT,
WE WILL MAINTAIN OUR STANDARD OF INNOVATION AND
INCLUSIVENESS BY PUBLISHING HIGHLY ORIGINAL POETRY
FROM ACCROSS THE CULTRUAL SPECTRUM, REFLECTING
OUR LONGSTANDING COMMITMENT TO THIS MOST
ANCIENT AND STUBBORNLY ENDURING FORM OF ART.

CITY LIGHTS SPOTLIGHT

1

Norma Cole, *Where Shadows Will:*
Selected Poems 1988-2008

2

Anselm Berrigan, *Free Cell*

3

Andrew Joron, *Trance Archive:*
New and Selected Poems

4

Cedar Sigo, *Stranger in Town*

5

Will Alexander, *Compression & Purity*